Alcoholic FAMILY DISORDERS

About the authors:

Roy W. Pickens, Ph.D., is a professor of psychology in the Department of Psychiatry at the University of Minnesota Medical School. He has been a consultant to Hazelden since 1978.

Dace S. Svikis, B.A., is a graduate student in the Clinical Psychology Division of the Department of Psychology at the University of Minnesota. She is presently receiving training in clinical research at Hazelden.

Alcoholic FAMILY DISORDERS

MORE THAN STATISTICS

Roy W. Pickens and Dace S. Svikis

Hazelden

First published March, 1985.

ISBN: 0-89486-258-8

Printed in the United States of America.

Editor's Note:
Hazelden Educational Materials offers a variety of information on chemical dependency and related areas. Our publications do not necessarily represent Hazelden or its programs, nor do they officially speak for any Twelve Step organization.

CONTENTS

1

INTRODUCTION

In dealing with alcoholism, our attention is focused primarily on the problems of the alcoholic. This is as it should be, for unless the alcoholic admits to his or her problems and is willing to take the necessary steps to resolve them, recovery is not possible. However, it is common to see other family members focus on these problems as well, out of concern for the alcoholic's recovery. While this focus may benefit the recovering person, it is important to remember that *if we focus exclusively on the alcoholic's problems, we may fail to recognize problems developing in other family members.*

What are the problems that affect alcoholic families? They can be many and varied, and in some ways resemble those that affect nonalcoholic families. However, a group of these problems, termed *alcoholic family disorders,* are of special concern to such families. These are disorders that occur more frequently in families of alcoholics than in others, and therefore are a special risk. Unfortunately, this increased risk is frequently unknown by relatives of alcoholics because of a lack of information about such disorders.

The purpose of this pamphlet is to provide information on the nature and characteristics of alcoholic family disorders, and to sensitize us to the problems that may develop in other members of the family. The pamphlet is addressed to the relatives of alcoholics, alcoholics themselves, and others who wish to know more about these problems. It is not written to divert attention from the alcoholic's problems, for we must be concerned about and continue to focus on such problems. It is written in the belief that if alcoholic family problems are recognized and dealt with effectively, a large amount of unnecessary pain and suffering can be avoided.

When reading this material, be forewarned about one important point. For the most part, we will discuss findings that pertain to families of alcoholics in general. While these findings will be true for such families as a group, they will not necessarily apply to every person within that group. For example, relatives of alcoholics may have a higher rate of a particular problem than relatives of nonalcoholics. This does not mean that all relatives of alcoholics will develop the problem. Some will develop it while others will not. Keep this firmly in mind while reading the following material.

2

DISORDERS OF ALCOHOLIC FAMILIES

Disorders in alcoholic families are mostly psychiatric in nature, and these people tend to have more emotional and behavioral disturbances than nonalcoholics. The most common disorders in alcoholic families are alcoholism, depression, and sociopathy. Other disorders that occur less frequently (but still occur more often than in other families) are hysteria, eating disorders, and the hyperactive child syndrome. Finally, the fetal alcohol syndrome is a disorder that occurs only in children of mothers who drink alcohol.

Alcoholic family disorders that typically make their first appearance during adulthood are alcoholism, depression, and hysteria. Alcoholism is a severe disorder with which most relatives of alcoholics are familiar because they have seen the disorder develop. However, people who have had limited exposure to alcoholism are sometimes surprised to hear the disease runs in families. These people incorrectly assume that because of an awareness of problems that alcoholism creates, relatives of alcoholics would be less likely to drink.

Depression is another alcoholic family disorder, one which primarily affects a person's mood or emotions. Depressed people are unhappy, show little interest in doing things, and appear to get little satisfaction out of life. This is a serious disorder that can be debilitating and, if left untreated, may lead a person to suicide.

The third adult alcoholic family disorder is hysteria, in which a person may have a wide range of medical problems for which no physical cause can be found. This is because the problems are of psychological rather than physical origin. Hysterics are typically constant complainers and are unwilling to accept a psychological basis for their problems.

During adolescence, alcoholic family disorders that may appear are sociopathy and eating disorders. With sociopathy, the person is self-centered and has little regard for others' feelings. Sociopaths reject authority and bend the rules as necessary to achieve their desires. People with this disorder often have job problems and sometimes experience legal problems as well.

Eating disorders include anorexia nervosa and bulimia. Anorexia is a disorder in which the person develops an aversion to eating and becomes skinny and malnourished. Sometimes anorectics die from medical complications of their starvation diets. Bulimics are people who have lost control over their eating but are obsessed with not gaining weight. They eat a large amount of food in a short period of time and maintain normal weight by forcing vomiting afterwards.

Alcoholic family disorders that may appear during childhood are the fetal alcohol and the hyperactive child syndromes. The fetal alcohol syndrome is a condition in which the child is born with a characteristic set of physical deformities and is mentally retarded. With the hyperactive child syndrome, a child may be hyperactive, impulsive, and have difficulty attending to tasks for normal periods of time. This disorder frequently causes school and adjustment problems for the child.

We know each of these disorders occurs more frequently in families of alcoholics, but why they do so isn't clearly understood. When more information is available, perhaps effective means can be developed for preventing such problems, and these families will be able to lead more normal lives. For now, we must try to minimize the occurrence of these disorders and the problems they may cause.

3

ADULT RELATIVES OF ALCOHOLICS

Alcoholism, depression, and hysteria are alcoholic family disorders that develop primarily in adults. Alcoholism is the most common. For men, alcoholism usually develops when they are in their late teens or early twenties. For women, however, the development may be somewhat later. Usually depression first develops when the person is around age 40, although it can appear much earlier or later. Hysteria usually begins during early adulthood (typically before age 30).

Alcoholism

Once an alcoholic is found in a family, it is likely other alcoholics will be found in that same family. How often does this occur? For a long time we thought about one-third of all alcoholics had a close relative who was also alcoholic.[1] Now we think well over one-half of all alcoholics have a close relative (parent, sibling, or child) who is also alcoholic. When more distant relatives are included (grandparents, aunts/uncles, and nephews/nieces), the number of alcoholics who have at least one alcoholic relative is increased to almost 70%.[2] Therefore, it is more likely that an alcoholic will, rather than will not, have a relative with the disease. Often the disease is seen in many members of the same family, and extends across several generations. For this reason, alcoholism is frequently described as a "family disease."

In a recent study of family alcoholism conducted at Hazelden, we found that as many as 38% of close relatives of alcoholics are problem drinkers. Since national surveys show the rate of problem drinking to be about 5-10% in the general population, this indicates that the rate of problem drinking in relatives of alcoholics is about four times higher than the national average.

When alcoholism occurs in a family, it is most often the father, brother, or son who is alcoholic; although it can be the mother, sister, or daughter. Alcoholism occurs two to three times more often in males than in females.

Female alcoholics tend to report more alcoholic relatives than do male alcoholics. This is particularly the case for female relatives (mothers, sisters, daughters) of female alcoholics. Why this is true isn't understood. Perhaps the alcoholism rates for relatives of male and female alcoholics are actually the same but women are more sensitive to drinking problems in their relatives. Alcoholic women would then report more alcoholism in their relatives than would alcoholic men.

We indicated before that as many as one-half of all alcoholics may have a close alcoholic relative. This means that in the other half, the disease develops in a person without developing in other family members. This is an important point for family members: just because one person is alcoholic we should not expect other family members to necessarily become alcoholic.

In terms of future risks to children in the family, we would like to predict if alcoholism that develops in a person is the "family" or "nonfamily" type. Unfortunately, this determination cannot be made with certainty. We may be able to make an educated guess by examining the drinking history of other members in the family. If alcoholism is not found among other family members, it is likely that children in the family will not necessarily have a higher risk for developing alcoholism. However, if alcoholism is found in other family members, this suggests that children in the family may be at increased risk for developing alcoholism. Keep in mind these are only guesses and not facts.

People are sometimes surprised to hear that alcoholics frequently have other alcoholic relatives. One would expect the opposite to be true; that is, firsthand experience with the adverse consequences drinking has had on one family member should encourage the rest of the family to vow never to drink. While it is true that other family members often react by not drinking or by being very careful about the amount they drink, all too often the opposite occurs and those people eventually become alcoholic. How this happens will be discussed in a later section of this pamphlet.

Depression

Another disorder that tends to run in families of alcoholics is depression. Psychiatrists and psychologists frequently call this condition a major depressive illness. Regardless of what it is called, depression is primarily a disturbance that affects how people feel (their mood or emotional state) and ranges from mild to severe cases. People who are depressed feel unhappy or "blue," and lack an interest in doing things or no longer like to do things they once found enjoyable. They may cry easily and complain of feeling worthless or helpless. Overall, they find it a chore just getting through each day.

Depressed people frequently have trouble concentrating on their work or paying attention to a conversation. In terms of behavioral changes, some depressed people display a lack of energy while others are irritable and agitated. In more severe cases, the person may also show changes in eating and sleeping habits. Some people tend to eat more as they become depressed and gain significant amounts of weight. Others may lose their appetites and experience a significant weight loss. Similar changes may occur in sleep patterns, with some depressed people sleeping more while others have trouble sleeping.

Everyone gets depressed on occasion. For this reason psychiatrists and psychologists usually distinguish between situational depression and a depressive illness. Situational depression is when a person experiences a period of sadness caused by a specific unfortunate event, such as the death of a close family member, loss of a job, or divorce. In such cases, if the cause of depression is known and does not persist beyond a reasonable period of time, it is not viewed as abnormal. However, if there is no cause for the depression and the person shows a number of depressive symptoms that persist for more than several weeks, then the condition is not normal and may be a mental disorder. In such cases, the person is encouraged to seek some type of professional help.

It is estimated that approximately 15% of all people will experience a major depressive illness at some point in their lives. Women are twice as likely as men to become depressed, with a rate of about 20%. Depression is usually treated effectively by psychotherapy and/or antidepressant medication.

Alcoholics tend to have higher rates of depression than the general population. Some studies have found that as many as 50% of all alcoholics are depressed when admitted to treatment programs.[3] Of course, this excessive rate of depression is related in part to the person's alcoholism. It is not unusual for a number of serious problems to develop by the time the alcoholic enters treatment. If these problems are obviously the cause of the depression then the depression is situational (i.e., caused by specific unfortunate events associated with alcoholism). This depression lessens with treatment for alcoholism, as the person begins to resolve some of the problems caused by the disease.

In other cases, depression associated with alcoholism is thought to be a depressive illness. For these alcoholics, the depressed mood does not improve with alcoholism treatment, and may even worsen. In a depressive illness, the person continues to be depressed long after the problems caused by alcoholism are resolved. For these people, there is often clear evidence of depression existing before the onset of alcoholism, which may have played a role in developing the alcoholism. Depressed people are more likely to develop alcoholism if their motivation for drinking was to reduce the depressive symptoms. Such depression should be recognized and treated as part of the person's alcoholism treatment program. If untreated, the depression may lead the person to relapse after treatment.

Depression also occurs at a high rate among relatives of alcoholics. This occurs whether the relative is alcoholic or not, and is a particular risk for female relatives. While the rate of depression among male relatives is approximately the same as males in the general population (about 10%), the rate of depression among female relatives (about 40%) is almost twice as high as females in the general population (about 20%). This is particularly true for female relatives of female alcoholics, where almost 50% of these relatives will become depressed at some time during their lives.[4]

The causes of depression in relatives of alcoholics are thought to be similar to the causes in alcoholics themselves. Some of the depression may be situational, with the relative reacting normally to the problems of living with an alcoholic. This should also improve after the alcoholic begins treatment. Other types of depression in relatives may reflect a depressive illness. In such cases, it may have existed before the development of alcoholism in another family member. This depression will not necessarily improve with the alcoholic entering treatment. In either case, professional help is necessary for the affected person if the depressive symptoms are severe and persist for more than a few weeks. Failure to recognize and seek help for depressive problems would be unfortunate, as treatment is effective and will improve the quality of the depressed person's life.

When depression develops in a member of a family, it affects not only that person but other family members as well. At first, relatives usually do not recognize the disorders as depression. Instead, they think the person is discouraged, acting grouchy, or "out of sorts." However, if the symptoms of depression become more severe, family members are likely to become aware of the person's emotional problems. At this time the family may become more supportive and attempt to cheer up the person. As the symptoms persist, however, some family members may lose patience and actually blame the person for the depressed behavior. It is important for family members to recognize depression as an emotional disorder, and that depressed relatives are not responsible for all of their actions.

When a member of an alcoholic family is depressed, the consequences can be particularly severe and may cause additional stress for the alcoholic. For the untreated alcoholic, this might be reflected in increased drinking or a temptation to use the depressed person's behavior as an excuse for drinking. For the recovering alcoholic, the stress might increase the likelihood of relapse. Not only does depression in the family cause additional problems for the alcoholic, but alcoholism in the family also causes problems for the depressed person. Because of a tendency to focus on his or her own problems, the alcoholic is often not able to give the depressed person the necessary emotional support. In such cases, understanding and support of other family members is then needed by both the alcoholic and depressed person.

In any family, depression is not a condition to be taken lightly. Depressed people typically feel worthless and irritable, and frequently think of dying. When someone is severely depressed, the risk of suicide increases dramatically. One study found 75% of all suicide victims were depressed at the time of the act.[5] All too often the family doesn't recognize the seriousness of the problem.

Hysteria

Another disorder that can affect family members of alcoholics is hysteria. Other names used by psychiatrists and psychologists for this disorder are Briquet's syndrome and somatization disorder. The word "hysteria" makes people think of uncontrollable, highly excitable, and overly emotional behavior. Actually, hysteria is a form of psychiatric illness in which a person experiences a large number of physical symptoms, but no physical cause can be found. Rather, psychological factors are responsible for the symptoms. Nonetheless, the person with the disorder experiences a great deal of pain and discomfort.

Hysterics may show many different types of physical problems, including gastrointestinal difficulties (upset stomach, vomiting, stomach pain, bloating), menstrual irregularities (painful menstrual periods, severe cramps, excessive bleeding), sexual problems (pain during intercourse, lack of interest in sex), body aches and pains (back pain, neck pain), dizziness, shortness of breath, blurred vision, trouble swallowing, fainting, etc.[6] Hysteria is generally thought of as an anxiety-related disorder. People with this disorder may be unable or unwilling to admit feeling anxious. When this happens, the anxiety is expressed in the form of physical symptoms.[7]

Hysterics frequently seek medical treatment for their physical problems. Unable to find a physical cause for the hysteric's symptoms, doctors become frustrated. Referring such patients to psychological treatment may be extremely difficult, because hysterics tend to deny having psychological problems. They are firmly convinced their problems result from purely physical causes. Thus, they refuse to seek psychological help, preferring to "doctor shop" and obtain treatment from more than one physician.

It is important to note that while each of us has probably at some point during our lives experienced some of the problems listed above, this does not warrant a diagnosis of hysteria. Rather, people with hysteria experience physical symptoms that are chronic in nature. The symptoms persist for longer periods of time and are much more difficult to treat effectively. This should not be interpreted to mean that hysterics are lying or faking their symptoms. The symptoms are real and often cause considerable discomfort, but they originate from psychological rather than physical causes.

Hysteria occurs almost exclusively in women at a rate of 1% in the general population. In order to diagnose hysteria, several chronic physical symptoms with no known physical cause must be identified.[8]

While many of the physical symptoms can be treated by the family physician, relief is often short-lived. Medication and other forms of medical therapy treat only the physical symptoms of the disorder. They do not address the psychological issues of what may be causing the symptoms. While medical treatment may provide temporary relief, treatment of the psychological factors underlying the symptoms is much more difficult and has met with only limited success. The biggest obstacle in treating hysteria is the hysteric's reluctance to admit to having psychological problems.

The relationship between hysteria and alcoholism has received considerable attention, for it appears the two disorders occur often in the same family. For example, the rate of alcoholism in family members of hysterics is much higher than the 5-10% rate in the general population. One study found that nearly one-fourth of all relatives of hysterics are alcoholic.[9] Therefore, the risk for hysteria would be higher for members of alcoholic families.

Hysterics are concerned and preoccupied with their symptoms, and frequently seek reassurances from family members and friends about their physical problems. Because of the chronic nature of the disorder, relatives and friends often think hysterics are constant complainers and eventually stop listening to their problems. Thus, in an effort to maintain the attention of others, hysterics sometimes dramatize and exaggerate their symptoms. It is important that family members understand the nature of hysteria and not hold the hysteric responsible for his or her symptoms. Above all, family members should not avoid contact with hysterics because of their constant complaining. However, family members should also not shower hysterics with attention and listen endlessly to their complaints. Instead, family members should maintain a positive and constructive attitude around the hysteric. Above all else, they should encourage the hysteric to seek psychological help for his or her problem, if such help is recommended by a physician.

In many ways, the problems of living with a hysteric are similar to those of living with a depressed person. The hysteric's intense concern and preoccupation with his or her symptoms and a constant need for reassurance can be emotionally stressful to other members of the family. Also, frequent medical visits resulting in temporary treatment of the hysteric's symptoms are not only frustrating and stressful to the family, but can also cause considerable financial difficulties.

When both alcoholism and hysteria occur in different members of the same family, the stress placed upon the family is increased even more. Hysterics are usually so concerned about their own physical problems that they are unable to provide an alcoholic family member with the emotional support he or she needs. Also, untreated alcoholics may react to their frustration and inability to help the hysteric by increasing the amount they drink. Understanding and help of other family members is greatly needed in such cases.

CHAPTER 3
ENDNOTES

[1]N.S. Cotton, "The Familial Incidence of Alcoholism: A Review," *Journal of Studies on Alcohol,* Volume 40 (1979), pp. 89-116.

[2]M.A. Schuckit, F.N. Pitts, T. Reich, L.J. King, and G. Winokur, "Alcoholism: I. Two Types of Alcoholism in Women," *Archives of General Psychiatry,* Volume 20 (1969), pp. 301-306.

[3]R. Cadoret and G. Winokur, "Depression in Alcoholism," *Annals of the New York Academy of Sciences,* Volume 233 (1974), pp. 34-39.

[4]G. Winokur, J. Rimmer, and T. Reich, "Alcoholism IV: Is There More Than One Type of Alcoholism?" *British Journal of Psychiatry,* Volume 118 (1971), pp. 525-531.

[5]C.V. Leonard, "Depression and Suicidality," *Journal of Consulting and Clinical Psychology,* Volume 42 (1974), pp. 98-104.

[6]American Psychiatric Association, *Diagnostic and Statistical Manual of Mental Disorders* (DSM-III), Third Edition (Washington, D.C., American Psychiatric Association, 1980).

[7]J.C. Coleman, J.N. Butcher, and R.C. Carson, *Abnormal Psychology and Modern Life,* Seventh Edition (Glenview, Illinois, Scott, Foresman and Co., 1984).

[8]*Ibid.*

[9]P.I. Woerner and S.B. Guze, "A Family and Marital Study of Hysteria," *British Journal of Psychiatry,* Volume 114 (1968), pp. 161-168.

4

ADOLESCENT RELATIVES OF ALCOHOLICS

Sociopathy and eating disorders are alcoholic family disorders that may develop in adolescent relatives of alcoholics. Sociopathy typically begins before age fifteen or sixteen, while eating disorders usually develop during the middle adolescent years.

Sociopathy

Psychiatrists and psychologists also refer to this disorder as antisocial personality disorder and psychopathic personality disorder. As is evident by the emphasis on "personality" in these names, sociopathy is not confined to a limited period of illness like depression. Rather, it is a long-term pattern of behavior involving difficulties in living with other people and society that extends throughout the person's lifetime. These people are called sociopaths or psychopaths.

Sociopaths are generally self-centered people willing to bend the rules as necessary to achieve their desires. Such people like excitement and live only in the present, without regard to either the future or the past. They have a low tolerance for frustration and willingly exploit others in their drive to obtain immediate personal gratification. They also reject authority and are unable to profit from past experience. Because they are usually not affected by feelings of anxiety or guilt, sociopaths often do things other people would avoid. Thus, they frequently have problems in personal relationships and in adjusting to the rules, regulations, and laws required by schools, jobs, and communities.

When first met, sociopaths are likeable people, appearing charming, amusing, and sincere. Because of this and their need for excitement, they make friends easily and are fun to be around. However, their shallowness and self-centeredness become evident later. As the need suits them, they become manipulative and deceitful to satisfy their desires. This causes considerable problems for others, and when confronted with their own behavior, sociopaths act innocent or project blame onto others. Sociopaths never admit they are at fault for the problems they have caused. Emotionally, they tend not to understand the true meaning of close personal relationships. They can be irresponsible and unfaithful and, although frequently promising to change, rarely do.[1]

Like depression, sociopathy may range in severity from mild to severe. In the general population, sociopathy occurs more frequently in males (3%) than in females (1%). Among females the disorder typically becomes evident at puberty, while in males it may appear earlier in childhood. Lying, stealing, fighting, and truancy are early symptoms of the disorder. As the person gets older, alcohol and other drug abuse, sexual promiscuity, and occupational and legal problems may develop.[2]

A significant number of sociopaths are eventually placed in prisons and correctional institutions. This is especially true for the "hostile psychopath," who often gets newspaper attention for crimes committed. But most sociopaths never come to the attention of the law. Nevertheless, many live on the fringes of the law, engaging in unscrupulous business practices, becoming crooked politicians, etc. In terms of treatment, sociopathy is a disorder that is difficult to correct. There is no effective medication to treat the disorder, and sociopaths are very resistant to treatment by psychotherapy. Fortunately, many tend to improve beginning around the age of 40, when they start to "burn out."

Because of their like of excitement and desire for immediate personal gratification, sociopaths are likely to abuse alcohol as well as other drugs. Along with depression, sociopathy is one of the most common disorders seen in people being admitted for alcoholism treatment. Sociopathic men are almost three times more likely to be alcoholic than emotionally healthy men. Sociopathic women are almost five times more likely to be alcoholic than emotionally healthy women. Sociopathic men and women have a higher rate of dual dependency, even higher than for a dependency on alcohol alone.[3]

Why is sociopathy so closely associated with alcoholism? In one sense, alcoholism may cause a person to behave sociopathically. Alcohol reduces inhibitions and often makes people say and do things they would not ordinarily do. Alcoholism also causes considerable stress for the alcoholic, which may lead to irrational and self-centered behavior. Therefore, when alcoholism is the primary problem, treatment for the alcoholism would be effective in eliminating much of the sociopathic behavior. On the other hand, sociopaths are not overly concerned about the consequences of their behavior. They may begin to experiment early with alcohol and other drugs, which can lead to chemical dependence. And when sociopathy is the primary problem, treating the person for alcoholism would not have much effect on the sociopathic behavior. These people tend to be "perfect patients" in alcoholism treatment programs and then relapse shortly after leaving treatment.

Not only is sociopathy likely to exist along with alcoholism in the same person, but sociopathy is also likely to exist among the alcoholic's family. This is particularly true for male relatives of alcoholics, where sociopathy is twice as common (6%) as that seen among males in the general population (3%). While these percentages are small and seemingly do not account for a large number of people, the amount of sociopathy seen among specific types of alcoholics is much higher. For example, let's look at male alcoholics who are also sociopathic (which is estimated to include about

20% of all male alcoholics). For this group, the rate of sociopathy among male relatives is 22%, which is seven times more than reported in the general population.[4]

When sociopathy occurs among relatives of alcoholics, the consequences can be severe for the other family members. The problems may begin in middle childhood when the sociopath has disciplinary problems with authority figures (i.e., teachers, parents). Lying, stealing, and fighting may also be evident during this time. These problems may increase during middle adolescence with alcohol and other drug experimentation and sexual promiscuity. Legal problems may start to arise and the person may have difficulty holding a job after becoming an adult. All of these activities will cause stress to the alcoholic and his or her family. If this stress is not dealt with effectively, it may become a detrimental factor in the alcoholic's recovery.

While little is available in effective treatment for the sociopath, counseling can help family members. Family counseling can help minimize problems caused by the sociopath, as well as teach family members how to deal with the sociopath to minimize the severity of the disorder.

Eating Disorders

Eating disorders such as bulimia and anorexia nervosa are also seen in families of alcoholics. Bulimia involves rapid eating of large amounts of food within a very short period of time, often followed by self-induced vomiting. Although some bulimics eat as many at 50,000 calories during a single eating binge, most consume between 3,000 and 10,000 calories per binge. In a single eating binge, bulimics may consume from one to three times the number of calories the average person eats in one day. Most binge foods are high in calories and include cookies, donuts, potato chips, chocolate, ice cream, pizza, bread, and other sweet and/or salty foods high in carbohydrates. Bulimics typically binge eat only when alone, with binges lasting from one to two hours and often occurring during the evening.

The important issue in bulimia is not how much a person eats nor the types of foods eaten. Rather, it is the loss of control over eating. Bulimics fear that once they start to eat they will be unable to stop. They are also preoccupied with food. In many ways, the loss of control and obsession with food experienced by bulimics closely resembles the obsession alcoholics have with alcohol. The inability of bulimics to control eating and the realization that their eating pattern is abnormal, often leads to depression, anxiety, and low self-esteem.

Bulimia often begins during adolescence and early adulthood, and occurs 20 times more frequently in females than in males.[5] Many adolescent females experiment with binge eating and vomiting on at least one occasion. For some people, bulimia begins as a method of weight control. The benefits of being able to eat all you want while not gaining weight become very appealing, and a pattern of overeating followed by vomiting becomes established. Over time, the behavior may increase in frequency until some people binge eat and vomit several times a day. Other methods of weight control used by bulimics include excessive use of laxatives or diet pills, fasting (not eating at all for 24 hours or more), and compulsive exercise.

However, not all bulimics engage in methods of weight control; some only binge eat. They stop an eating binge only when they experience stomach pains, fall asleep, or are interrupted by family or friends. As might be expected, this subgroup of bulimics tend to become overweight. They may still experience the same psychological problems as those who vomit following an eating binge. Physically, however, *most* bulimics practice methods of weight control and therefore are generally of average or slightly below average weight.

People with bulimia are often reluctant to seek treatment. They feel guilty and ashamed about their abnormal eating behavior, and try to hide it from family and friends. They binge eat only in private and isolate themselves from others. To other family members, bulimics may appear physically healthy but somewhat moody, irritable, and unhappy. Bulimics may also feel down about themselves and tired all the time. Because of guilt and fear concerning their eating behavior, they are unable and unwilling to share their problems with family and friends. Therefore, family members become frustrated and angry about their inability to help the person with the disorder. This is understandable, but it is important for family members to provide a supportive home environment for the bulimic and encourage treatment for the disorder if it is recognized. Treatment is effective in reducing the frequency of the eating binges, and involves treating the binge eating first, and then focusing upon related issues and concerns.

Bulimics show a higher rate of alcoholism than the general population. Approximately one-fourth of bulimics have had previous treatment for alcoholism or other drug abuse.[6] (This rate of alcoholism is probably underestimated, since only those people who sought treatment were diagnosed. There is no way of knowing how many bulimics are alcoholics who have not had treatment.) Families of bulimics also show higher rates of alcoholism, with one-fourth to one-half of bulimics having at least one alcoholic relative.[7]

Anorexia nervosa is another eating disorder that occurs in alcoholic families. Primary symptoms of anorexia nervosa are an intense fear of becoming overweight and an unrelenting pursuit of thinness. People with this disorder typically lose from 25 to 50% of their original body weight. Some anorectics may lose so much that they end up weighing only 50 to 60 pounds. Despite their extreme thinness anorectics believe they are fat, and when asked to observe themselves in a mirror they don't see their skeleton-like appearance realistically.[8] Because of the high death rate (15-25%) in anorexia resulting from complications related to weight loss, intensive hospital treatment is usually required.

Anorexia nervosa occurs primarily in women and typically begins with a period of normal dieting during adolescence. Anorectics tend to be slightly overweight during early teen years, and dieting efforts are often encouraged by family and friends. However, as their dieting progresses and they achieve their original weight goal, they still believe they are fat. Thus, they revise their goals and set progressively lower target weights. Also, their diets become more restricted. What began as a sensible 1,500 calorie diet becomes a 600-800 calorie diet, considerably below the number of calories needed to maintain an average body weight. Anorectics particularly avoid such foods as bread, sweet rolls, and other desserts, eating primarily high protein and low carbohydrate foods such as fruits and vegetables.

It is important to realize that anorexia nervosa does not involve a loss of appetite. People with this disorder continue to experience intense hunger pains, but the fear of losing control over eating makes them avoid eating. Like bulimics, anorectics are preoccupied with food. They enjoy studying recipes and looking at pictures of food. They frequently cook for friends and family, but refuse to eat what they have prepared. Many also work in food-related jobs as waitresses and cooks.

Often the disorder comes to the attention of family and friends when the person has lost a considerable amount of weight and looks starved. Parents become concerned and try to make the anorectic eat. People with the disorder respond by saying, "I'm not hungry," or "I just ate at a friend's house." If forced to eat, anorectics quickly feel full and bloated. They also feel guilty about eating, and may induce vomiting to prevent weight gain. This is why some anorectics show bulimic symptoms and become bulimics, and vice versa.

Although the rate of alcoholism among anorectics is no different than in the general population, some studies have found that relatives of anorectics have a higher rate than the general population. One study found that 20% of all anorectics had at least one alcoholic relative.[9] This occurred primarily among anorectics who were also bulimic. This suggests that people with both anorexia and bulimia have higher rates of alcoholism in their families.[10]

CHAPTER 4
ENDNOTES

[1]J.C. Coleman, J.N. Butcher, and R.C. Carson, *Abnormal Psychology and Modern Life,* Seventh Edition (Glenview, Illinois, Scott, Foresman and Co., 1984).

[2]American Psychiatric Association, *Diagnostic and Statistical Manual of Mental Disorders* (DSM-III), Third Edition (Washington, D.C., American Psychiatric Association, 1980).

[3]C.E. Lewis, J. Rice, and J.E. Helzer, ''Diagnostic Interactions: Alcoholism and Antisocial Personality,'' *Journal of Nervous and Mental Disease,* Volume 171 (1983), pp. 105-113.

[4]G. Winokur, J. Rimmer, and T. Reich, ''Alcoholism IV: Is There More Than One Type of Alcoholism?'' *British Journal of Psychiatry,* Volume 118 (1971), pp. 525-531.

[5]American Psychiatric Association, 1980.

[6]R.L. Pyle, J.E. Mitchell, and E.D. Eckert, ''Bulimia: A Report of 34 Cases,'' *Journal of Clinical Psychiatry,* Volume 42 (1981), pp. 60-64.

[7]Pyle, Mitchell, and Eckert, 1981.
D.B. Herzog, ''Bulimia: The Secretive Syndrome,'' *Psychosomatics,* Volume 23 (1982), pp. 481-483.
J.I. Hudson, H.G. Pope Jr., J.M. Jonas, and D. Yurgelun-Tood, ''Family History Study of Anorexia Nervosa and Bulimia,'' *British Journal of Psychiatry,* Volume 142 (1983), pp. 133-138.

[8]P.E. Garfinkel and D.M. Garner, *Anorexia Nervosa: A Multidimensional Perspective* (New York, Brunner/Mazel, 1982).

[9]Herzog, 1982.

[10]Hudson, Pope Jr., Jonas, and Yurgelun-Todd, 1983.

5

CHILDREN OF ALCOHOLICS

Children of alcoholics can mature to have many of the same problems that affect their adult and adolescent relatives. These include an increased risk for developing alcoholism, depression, hysteria, sociopathy, and eating disorders previously described. However, problems of children of alcoholics are not limited just to their adult lives. They can also have more emotional and health problems during their childhood and adolescence than children of nonalcoholic parents.[1] Children of alcoholics show more problems with emotions, school, conduct, and the law than do other children.[2] In this section we will discuss two particularly severe disorders that may affect children of alcoholics during early development.

Fetal Alcohol Syndrome

Children with this disorder typically show a number of physical and behavioral abnormalities. In more severe cases, the syndrome can be easily recognized at birth. In milder cases, the syndrome may not be recognized until much later, perhaps only after the child has entered school. In very mild cases, the syndrome may escape detection altogether and never be recognized as a cause of a person's problems, since they fall within the normal range of these conditions in the general population.

In more recognizable cases of the syndrome, a distinct pattern of abnormalities is evident. At birth, affected children have a lower body weight and are smaller in size than the average child. While a child with the fetal alcohol syndrome may grow normally, lower body weight and smaller body size tend to persist throughout life. Another aspect of the syndrome is a characteristic facial appearance which consists of short eyelids, a low nasal bridge, a short upturned nose, and an absence of ridges between the nose and mouth. Altogether, facial features appear to be more closely concentrated in the center of the face than usual.

Behaviorally, children with the fetal alcohol syndrome (FAS) tend to be irritable and somewhat awkward in body movements. The most serious characteristic of FAS is the mental retardation that accompanies the low birth weight, distinct facial features, and poor coordination. The extent of mental retardation may range from mild to severe, and can be particularly debilitating to a child in school. In some children with the syndrome, mental retardation is so severe they cannot profit from a normal classroom experience. In other cases the mental retardation is not so severe, and the children can attend school normally but will have much trouble with school work.[3]

What is the cause of FAS? The disorder is thought to be caused by the pregnant mother's use of alcohol during the child's prenatal stage. Ordinarily, as the fetus is developing in the mother's uterus, it is protected by a placental barrier from contact with a large number of substances taken by the pregnant mother. However, alcohol drunk by a pregnant woman readily crosses the placental barrier, and can interfere with the fetus' normal development. The result is that the fetus is born with abnormalities of body structures and functions. The fetal alcohol syndrome is the name given to the characteristic set of abnormalities caused by alcohol on the developing fetus.

Children born to alcoholic women are at high risk for having FAS because of the large amounts of alcohol drunk during pregnancy. At one time it was not clear if alcohol itself was the cause of the syndrome or if it was some other factor typically associated with alcoholism (for example, nutritional deficiencies or cigarette smoking). Recently, the role of alcohol in the development of the disorder has been clearly established. There is no longer any doubt that alcohol consumed by a pregnant woman can have severe consequences for her developing child, especially if the alcohol is consumed in large amounts.

Since FAS occurs during pregnancy, children of men who drink are not at risk for having the disorder. Similarly, children of women who do not drink alcohol during pregnancy are not at risk. Women who consume large amounts of alcohol while pregnant are more likely to have children with the disorder than women who drink slight amounts. However, it is not known for certain how much alcohol will cause fetal alcohol syndrome. Because of large differences in how people respond to alcohol and the fear that even small amounts of alcohol may produce subtle harm to the fetus, some women have wisely elected to drink no alcohol during pregnancy.

Not all chronic alcoholic women have children with FAS. Several investigators have found that about 30% of all children born to chronic alcoholic women show evidence of the disorder. At present we do not know why the disorder develops in children of some but not all alcoholic women. Thus, while this means the majority of children born to alcoholic women do not show any such signs, the severity of the problems associated with the disorder should encourage all alcoholic women to seek treatment before pregnancy.

Hyperactive Child Syndrome

This is another disorder that occurs more often in children of alcoholics than in children of nonalcoholics. The disorder may first be noticeable when the child is three years of age. However, the symptoms often go unrecognized by parents during early childhood, and the disorder is identified by teachers after the child starts school.

Children with hyperactivity always appear to be "on the go," and show aimless activity, running, and fidgeting. As a result, they appear restless and unable to sit still for long periods of time. Another characteristic is that hyperactive children are easily distracted and find it difficult to concentrate on projects or activities. Their behavior tends to be haphazard, poorly organized, and not goal-directed. A third symptom of the disorder is impulsivity. Hyperactive children often act without thinking, and shift their attention from one task to another without completing any activity.

These problems of lack of attention, hyperactivity, and impulsivity cause learning difficulties for the child in the classroom. Consequently, hyperactive children often fall behind in their schoolwork. Not only does the disorder cause social and educational problems for the child, it causes problems for those who are working with the child as well. Socially, such children tend to talk constantly, but are shy around other children and act immature for their age.

Hyperactivity accounts for the greatest share of behavior problems among children in the elementary grades. However, it should be emphasized that hyperactive children do not necessarily show lower levels of intelligence. Their difficulties with school work are related primarily to distractability, impulsivity, and excessive activity. As might be imagined, learning and behavior problems of the hyperactive child also cause a considerable amount of distress for parents and other family members.

Psychiatrists and psychologists who work with hyperactive children also call this condition an attention deficit disorder, although children can show a deficit of attention without being hyperactive. Treatment involves daily administration of medicines that stimulate activity of the brain (Dexedrine or Ritalin). These medicines have a calming effect on hyperactive children, decreasing hyperactivity and distractability while at the same time increasing attention span and ability to concentrate. The symptoms usually disappear or are markedly reduced as the child enters the middle teens and early adulthood. In some cases the hyperactivity disappears, but the distractability and impulsivity persist into adult life.[4]

The hyperactive child syndrome occurs in the general population at a rate of 3%. It occurs about ten times more frequently in boys than in girls. Alcoholics have a high rate of hyperactivity as children. One study found that 50% of a group of male alcoholics had symptoms of hyperactivity during childhood.[5] This suggests that hyperactivity may have been a factor in the child's later development of alcoholism. It is clear that hyperactivity runs in alcoholic families, and may be a special problem to children of alcoholics. Parents of hyperactive children are about twice as likely to be alcoholic as parents of children who are not hyperactive.[6]

The hyperactive child syndrome can cause considerable problems for the affected family. The constant activity of such children can become especially tiresome for some parents. Because hyperactive children are easily distracted and impulsive, special learning programs must be employed by parents. The main goal of these programs is to help hyperactive children attend more to what they are doing and to be less impulsive in their actions. Parents of hyperactive children are usually advised to be consistent and straightforward when dealing with their children, and to apply rewards rather than punishment whenever possible. While stimulant medication can be effective in the control of hyperactive symptoms, such medication creates a special problem for alcoholic families. Many parents of hyperactive children worry about the possibility of abuse of the medication by the child or other family members. Access to the medication must be carefully monitored by parents. There is presently no evidence that use of this medication by hyperactive children predisposes them to future stimulant drug abuse.

CHAPTER 5
ENDNOTES

[1]R.W. Pickens, *Children of Alcoholics* (Center City, MN, Hazelden Foundation, 1984).

[2]C. Wilson and J. Orford, "Children of Alcoholics: Report of a Preliminary Study and Comments on the Literature," *Journal of Studies on Alcohol,* Volume 39 (1978), pp. 121-142.

[3]S. Landesman-Dwyer, "Drinking During Pregnancy: Effects on Human Development," *Alcohol and Health Monograph 2. Biomedical Processes and Consequences of Alcohol Use,* DHHS Publication No. (ADM) 82-1191 (1982), pp. 335-358.

[4]American Psychiatric Association, *Diagnostic and Statistical Manual of Mental Disorders* (DMS-III), Third Edition (Washington, D.C., American Psychiatric Association, 1980).

[5]D.W. Goodwin, F. Schulsinger, L. Hermansen, S.B. Guze, and G. Winokur, "Alcoholism and the Hyperactive Child Syndrome," *The Journal of Nervous and Mental Diseases,* Volume 160 (1975), pp. 349-353.

[6]J.R. Morrison and M.A. Stewart, "A Family Study of the Hyperactive Child Syndrome," *Biological Psychiatry,* Volume 3 (1971), pp. 189-195.

6

CAUSES OF ALCOHOLIC FAMILY DISORDERS

Why do depression, sociopathy, eating disorders, and hyperactivity tend to run in families with alcoholism? The answer to this question is not known. However, two factors are thought to be responsible. One is genetic, in which certain physical traits and behavioral tendencies are passed along from parent to child through inheritance. These are characteristics set at the moment of conception by the mixing of genes from the mother and father. We are all familiar with such characteristics, in which many people in a family have the same hair color, facial features, or body build. The other factor is environmental, in which life experiences may alter a person's physical features and behavioral tendencies. These experiences also begin at the moment of conception and extend throughout the person's life. Education is an example of an environmental factor that influences a person's life, as is the early rearing environment created by the family.

Several environmental factors may account for the occurrence of alcoholism and the other disorders within the same family. First, a disorder may develop in a person in reaction to a family member's alcoholism. (Alcoholism can be very stressful.) If a person is unable to deal effectively with a relative's alcoholism, other disorders may develop as a consequence of that distress. Secondly, alcoholism may develop in reaction to one of the other disorders occurring in another family member. If a family member is sociopathic, for example, this may cause a considerable amount of distress for others. Some may attempt to deal with this stress by drinking more alcohol, which can predispose such people to alcoholism. Both examples would act as environmental factors in the development of alcoholism and other disorders within members of the same family.

In other cases, alcoholism, depression, sociopathy, eating disorders, and hyperactivity may be genetically related. Genetic factors are believed to be at least partially involved in the transmission of alcoholism within the family. Children born of alcoholic parents but adopted at an early age and reared by nonalcoholic parents will have the same rate of alcoholism as children born and reared by alcoholic parents.[1] The genetic factors responsible for alcoholism may be linked to those responsible for the development of the other disorders. When one disorder occurs in a family it is likely that others will occur as well. Thus, the family unit would provide genetic as well as environmental factors necessary to develop alcoholism and other disorders.

Since these disorders run in the same families, it may be that they are, in fact, different manifestations of the same basic disease. To date, no one has speculated on the nature of this basic disease, although its existence has been suggested by several investigators in the field.[2] Hopefully, future research will shed light on these issues.

CHAPTER 6
ENDNOTES

[1]D.W. Goodwin, F. Schulsinger, N. Moller, et al., "Drinking Problems in Adopted and Nonadopted Sons of Alcoholics," *Archives of General Psychiatry,* Volume 31 (1974), pp. 164-169.

[2]G. Winokur, J. Rimmer, and T. Reich, "Alcoholism IV: Is There More Than One Type of Alcoholism?" *British Journal of Psychiatry,* Volume 118 (1971), pp. 525-531.

7

TREATMENT AND PREVENTION

Besides alcoholism, there are many other disorders in alcoholic families, as we have discussed. We know these disorders are often not recognized by the general public or members of alcoholic families, and are primarily psychiatric in nature. We also know the incidence of these disorders is several times higher in alcoholic families than in other families, or in the general population.

Since various disorders can be a reaction to the problems caused by alcoholism in the family, treatment of the alcoholic for alcoholism may be helpful in alleviating the other problems. On the other hand, if alcohol is being used to alleviate symptoms of the other disorders, then treatment for these disorders when they first appear may prevent the later development of alcoholism. In people already alcoholic, treatment for these other disorders should be made part of every alcoholism treatment program. This would reduce the chances of the person relapsing after treatment.

Since other disorders in alcoholic families can be a consequence of one family member's alcoholism, it is important that the alcoholic receive prompt and effective treatment for the disease. This has significant implications both in terms of treatment and prevention of these disorders in other family members. If the disease can be stopped, the chances of other disorders developing in the relatives of the alcoholic will be diminished. In the case of FAS, it will be entirely prevented.

In the treatment of disorders within alcoholic families, one must be concerned about the use of medication. If medication is prescribed, what is the likelihood that the person will abuse or become dependent on it? Since members of alcoholic families in general have an increased tendency to abuse drugs, this is a possibility that must be considered in selecting the type of treatment. Not all types of behavioral disorders require the use of medication. However, some medications can be useful in the treatment of behavioral disorders. For the most part, such medication has a low potential for abuse. However, some types of medication can lead to substantial amounts of abuse, and this may be a particular problem for members of alcoholic families. If at all possible, the use of medication with high abuse potential should be avoided in the treatment of alcoholic family members. In such cases, the physician should be fully informed as to the nature of the alcoholic family history before prescribing any medication. This would permit selection of the safest and most effective treatment and would allow the patient's use of the medication to be carefully monitored during treatment.

After reading the previous chapters, you may be aware that a member of your family is developing or already has developed one of the problems discussed. If such is the case, you should encourage that person to seek immediate professional help. Many of the problems described here can be treated successfully, especially if detected early. Disorders for which there is effective treatment include alcoholism and other drug addiction, depression, hyperactivity, and eating disorders. Unfortunately, treatment outcome is less effective for sociopathy and hysteria, but hopefully better treatment will be developed in the future. Also, no treatment is available for FAS, since it is primarily a developmental disorder.

While it is not possible to prevent alcoholism from developing in other family members, all alcoholic families should be warned of their increased risks for developing the disease and be encouraged to be extremely cautious if they choose to drink. This is particularly true if several family members are alcoholic. If a person at risk for alcoholism never drinks, alcoholism cannot develop, regardless of the genetic role in the development of the disease. This will also help prevent many of the emotional problems caused by the alcoholic's drinking from developing in other family members.

8

AFTERWORD

We have written this pamphlet to provide you with information about alcoholic family disorders. This information was presented to give you knowledge and to help you, not alarm or cause distress.

If you are a member of an alcoholic family, the information contained in this pamphlet may distress you. You may be discouraged by these facts and feel helpless or angry. If you do, just remember that while there are a wide range of problems that run in alcoholic families, these problems are not the inevitable result of being a member of an alcoholic family. They may not ever affect you.

It is important to keep in mind that the majority of the problems discussed here occur at a relatively low rate in the general population. Although the rates at which these disorders develop in members of alcoholic families are several times higher, not every member of an alcoholic family will develop these disorders. In fact, they will affect only a portion of alcoholic families, and within these families, only a portion of individual family members.

While it is important to be aware of the possibility of these disorders, it is equally important not to become overly sensitive to them. While everyone at times may experience some of the symptoms described above, showing these symptoms occasionally is normal and should be of minimal cause for concern. However, if a number of the symptoms for a given disorder are present and continue for a month or more, some type of professional help is needed. It is important not to overreact to the possibility of these disorders developing in other family members. For example, if you are a member of an alcoholic family, don't let that influence your decision to marry or to have children. Rather, it should increase your awareness of the types of problems that can develop and help you recognize such problems should they occur.

The presence of alcoholic family disorders within a family is not a valid excuse for an alcoholic to continue drinking. To continue would be similar to a person with heart trouble not getting medical help because another member of the family also has severe heart trouble or other medical condition. It would be unfortunate if the reader thought the alcoholic were somehow to blame for the disorders in alcoholic families. The alcoholic is no more to blame for such problems than a depressed person is to blame for a family member's alcoholism.

We hope the information will make you sensitive to the needs of other members of alcoholic families in addition to the alcoholic. We also hope this information will make you better able to recognize the types of problems that can develop in alcoholic families. By being aware of these problems within alcoholic families, we can help the alcoholic and other family members as well.